Email Marketing & Artificial Intelligence

Copyright (c) 2024 by Catapult Press

All rights reserved.

No part of this publication may be reproduced, distributed, or transmitted in any form or by any means, including photocopying, recording, or other electronic or mechanical methods, without prior written permission of the publisher. One exception shall be brief quotations embedded in critical reviews or scholarly materials and cited appropriately.

First printing edition 2024

Legal Notice

The content herein is based on the author's research and expertise. The content herein may contain errors, reflect out-of-date understanding or contain other inaccuracies. No warranty or assurance of accuracy or correctness is stated or implied. The authors and contributors are not responsible for any errors or omissions.

Special Acknowledgement:

Matt Bacak extends particular thanks to each of the following contributors, without whom this volume would not exist:

Thomas Bleakney
Philip Booth
Jim Callahan
Chris Cordwell
Michelle Coughlin
Andrew D Cowan RN
Dennis N Durst
Rich Fedrizzi
Todd Geese
Sylvia Greinig
Tracy Grote
Steven Paul Harris
David "Howie" Howerton
True Shift Foundation

Daniel G Krueger
Jane M. Lengel
Dr. Adrian Low
Matt Luckman
Bernie Meyer
John Milic
Mary N Mirembe
Justin M Naylor
Charles Ra
Chad Schulte
Matt "Shappy" Shapiro
Dohn Thornton
Dan Ulin
Rob Wallace
Tiffany Wong

Contents

Introduction 9

Chapter 1: The Case for Email Marketing: Statistics, Spammers & Why Successful Marketers Can't Let Go 15

    Email Marketing & the "Almighty Dollar" .. 18

    Spammers Do What Spammers Do, But AI Can Help 21

Chapter 2: The "Grand Entrance" of Artificial Intelligence: A Little History 25

    A "Brief" History of Artificial Intelligence ... 29

    The "Face" of Today's AI is Constantly Changing 35

Chapter 3: The Intersection of Email Marketing & AI: Supporting the Email Ecosystem 39

    The 2 Kinds of Copywriters & How to Be the Right One 41

    Bringing AI Into the Equation 46

    A Brief Game Plan for Incorporating AI into Your Email Marketing 50

Chapter 4: The Nuts & Bolts of Using AI *or* Garbage in, Garbage Out, Pt. 1 53

    The Truth About Prompts & Talking to Artificial Intelligence 55

        Natural Language & AI "Conversation" .. 58

Keeping the "Conversation" Going with
Artificial Intelligence 61

   A Powerful Strategy for Affiliate
   Marketers 65

Your Quick Path to Artificial Intelligence
Marketing (Case Study)................................68

Chapter 5: The Nuts & Bolts of Solid Email Practice & Copy *or* Garbage In, Garbage Out, Pt. 2 77

   What's the Main Idea?................................79

   Short & Sweet Will Win the Day 86

      "You Gotta Have Style" 95

Chapter 6: Customization vs. Plagiarism 99

   3 Ways to Use AI, Create Custom Content,
   and Avoid Inadvertent Plagiarism 105

   It's Okay to Make Your Copy Your Own ...108

      Dior/Flannel Shirt Case Study on Making
      Copy Your Own..117

Chapter 7: Legal Issues You May Encounter with AI-Generated Content 123

   The Four Areas of IP Law...........................126

   False IP Claims 128

   False Product Claims 129

   Seek Legal Counsel 131

Chapter 8: Evaluating & Testing Results 133

Conclusion 138

Sources, References & Resources 139

Introduction

"There are lots of rules out there for writing good emails, but at the end of the day, the truth is it's only a good email if it gets opened. Otherwise, it's just a little bit of junk out there in the ether." – Steven Paul Harris

> **Email marketing and artificial intelligence may represent the most extraordinary and profitable union of old and new technologies that we have ever encountered.**

How's that for starting off with a bang?

By the way, the answer is *"Awesome."* *That's awesome* for starting off with a bang. And trust me, it is awesome <u>for you</u>, because by reading this book, you are getting an absolutely enormous head start in a race you might not have even known you were running otherwise.

You are getting a head start in the race to be among the email marketers who will still be standing (and generating wildly attractive returns) at the end of this decade (at the time of publication, that is less than six years away).

You need that head start because our industry is only going to get more competitive as the years pass.

You need that head start because the sharks are already circling in the water to feed on the email lists belonging to formerly successful (and now drowned) marketers who could not make the leap into 21st and 22nd century marketing strategies.

You need that head start because, hey, email marketing has a median $42: $1 return on investment, and it's always better to be way, way ahead of the median in this business[i].

So let's talk about that head start.

In this book, you will be introduced to what is probably the most powerful tool that an email marketer can ever add to their business. Whether you are just getting started or you have a well-established operation already, this tool has the potential to change everything. However, just like most tools, it can change everything for the better or for the worse.

Think about it: If I hand you a toolbox staple, like a hammer, and tell you to go out on the deck and deal with a loose board, you could use that hammer to change everything about deck repair for yourself (assuming you had never had access to a hammer before) because you would no longer have to pound in nails using the flat of your hand. On the other hand, you could use that hammer to change everything about deck repair for yourself (assuming you had never had access to a hammer before) by using it to bash your deck to pieces. It could go either way. I know which way I would *rather* it go, but we can agree: It *could* go either way.

Naturally, you want things to go the first way, wherein you have an incredibly positive experience using a hammer to fix your deck quickly and without injury, dramatically improving your overall deck-related productivity. This is what artificial intelligence (AI) can do for your email marketing business **if you use it correctly**. Used incorrectly, however, AI can bash your email marketing business to pieces – just like that hammer could be used to destroy your deck.

Those dual possibilities are why you need this book. This book is designed to help you use AI in your email marketing to make things go "the right way" rather than to bash your email marketing business to smithereens.

In this book, we will dive into why email marketing remains one of the best promotional models for a modern business, the history of AI and why that matters for you, the fascinating intersection (and possible collision) of the email marketing and AI worlds, the basics of highly effective copywriting with (and without) AI, and how to use AI to ramp up your email marketing game to heights you have never even imagined before.

It is time to take on the challenge and rise above your competition. It is time to bring your email marketing skills together with the most game-changing technology to emerge so far in this century.

Let's get started.

Matt Bacak

Chapter 1: The Case for Email Marketing: Statistics, Spammers & Why Successful Marketers Can't Let Go

""It's hard to believe it, but there has been a hard trend toward receiving emails from smartphone users in recent years. A lot of people tried to say email marketing was dead, but I think they were the people who did not really understand how to do it particularly well." – Mary N Mirembe, email marketer

In 2015, John Brandon, contributing editor of *Inc.com* and generally well-informed digital marketing expert, made a bold prediction. He warned readers that email would become obsolete by 2020, stating, "Stick a fork in your email – within five years, something else is going to replace it"[ii].

Brandon cited as justification for his prediction a myriad host of email-related inconveniences, including "weeding out important messages, fishing through enormous email chains trying to find one pesky link to a business plan, [and] the battle to get to inbox zero." He stated emphatically these issues and others like them would be the source of email's demise. He observed that in his own line of work, email had become "less and less important." He noted that his friends used Facebook to communicate instead of email. (Note: Since 2015, Facebook has been losing market share with younger users to TikTok, Instagram, SnapChat, and YouTube, although it still boasts about 3 billion users and conveniently announced in 2023 it would stop reporting this metric because, according to Facebook, it is "not relevant" to advertisers.[iii]) Finally, Brandon concluded email is a "black hole" because "people don't respond – or they take forever to respond" and "spam filters [have] become overly aggressive" and wrapped up with a resounding, "It's clear that many people don't even use email outside of work."

This was serious stuff, and, at the time, a lot of experts and analysts agreed with Brandon – at least on a gut level. In 2015, we all felt like it was possible email had taken us about as far as we could go and, in comparison to email, messaging on social networking on platforms like Facebook and Twitter was powered by rocket fuel. The world was not as disillusioned as it is today with social-media marketing, and the events of 2020 and the four years leading up to that presidential election had not yet created the pervasive and lasting aura of suspicion and intrigue around social networks that today affects both sides of the aisle and even the folks who have never voted in an American election in their lives.

It was a more innocent time, in some ways: a time during which it felt forward-thinking and even optimistic to say, "Email marketing is almost over," and begin looking ahead toward what might come next.

Fast forward 9 years, however...

...and you will find that Brandon misfired...big time.

> **Email marketing is alive, well, and making billions for those with the foresight not to drop it at the first whisper of endemicity.**

After all, when something is fully incorporated to the point that we take it for granted, that is when it truly starts to gain power. Email has certainly reached that point.

Email Marketing & the "Almighty Dollar"

"Only about one-third of professional marketers are still using email marketing, and yet revenue in this space reached $11 billion by the end of 2023," observed Sylvia Greinig, digital marketer, in a recent interview. She continued, "The question is, why are marketers leaving? The answer lies somewhere between intimidation and 'shiny object' syndrome."

This may be the most concise summary we have ever read of the email-marketing conundrum that has emerged since the industry adopted Brandon's take on its own death and started the final countdown to the end (by the way, for those of you keeping track, the ticker clicked over to "0" roughly 4 years ago by Brandon's count, and yet the email marketing industry has not imploded just yet, nor, to be clear, does it show any particular inclination to do so).

Check out just a few of the many statistics we have available (and many of which arrived via credible, successful, active email marketers who make it their business to send out news, research, and data like this in an email format) about email marketing in 2024:

- **There will be 4.6 billion email users by 2025[iv]**

- **Email use will continue post-2025 to grow by roughly 3% annually despite deep and pervasive market penetration[v]**

- **Email remains the most preferred channel for brand communications**

across all age-based demographics (Baby Boomers, Gen X, Millennial, Gen Z, and all associated overlap generations)[vi]

- **Nearly three-quarters of all respondents off all ages indicated they preferred email to other forms of communication because it is "more personal"**[vii]

- **The median return on investment for email marketing is $42: $1**[viii]

So, when you boil all of this down, you can reach an extremely attractive conclusion for yourself – assuming you are an email marketer. You can conclude that there is *more money* in our space than ever before and *fewer competitors* for that money.

Of course, it's unlikely to stay that way. One thing that is true for nearly all internet marketers across the spectrum, regardless of how they are using the internet to do their marketing, is that they are not afraid to pivot. As the more-money-less-competition truth becomes increasingly obvious, those marketers will pivot right back into email marketing. This industry is probably one of the most flexible industries out there, and you can be sure as the facts prove themselves out over the next few months and years, you will see a mass reentry into this space. The key to your success, then, will be to already have a position far, far ahead of the competition.

Spammers Do What Spammers Do, But AI Can Help

One of the most often-cited reasons for exiting the email marketing space by those who believe the medium is on its last legs is the explanation that spammers have just gotten too smart and too clever for the rest of us to handle. It is certainly true that email spam is ubiquitous, regardless of service provider and industry. In fact, more than half of all global email traffic is categorized as spam![ix] Not all of that classification is accurate or fair, however. Some of it could even be *your stuff*.

It used to be relatively easy to avoid having your emails categorized as spam. You simply avoided the use of dollar signs, the word "free," and several other "red flag" issues, and you were basically home free. Today, on the other hand, spammers are really good at creating emails that look (to automated filters, anyway) like well-meaning emails sent personally from one friend to another. As a result, spam filters have gotten tougher in an effort to keep "the baddies" out of your inbox.

Ha! We all know the truth about that! Sometimes, the "goodies" get lumped right in with "the baddies."

As a modern email marketer, you need the most powerful, insightful, and high-performance spam-avoidance data and direction available if you want to avoid the fallout from spammers undermining your credibility. That is one of the ways AI can help you, and it can do so using strategies that most email marketers – even the longstanding and most successful of them – simply do not understand.

"As time has passed in our industry, it has become increasingly the case that in email marketing, absolutely everything matters and, furthermore, everything is in a constant state of flux," said Dohn Thornton, digital marketer. Understanding not just that things are constantly changing and evolving but also *how* to get the most accurate information possible about the nature of these changes can make a huge difference in your ability to generate returns in your email marketing business. In fact, according to recent data released by Statista, the email marketing service industry (those providing services revolving around producing, analyzing, and distributing email marketing content), is currently valued at more than $7.5 billion and is expected to climb to nearly $18 billion by 2027[x]. Clearly, the powerhouses like Wal-Mart, Amazon, and Verizon, to name just a few dedicating multiple billions to the email marketing process annually, know how important it is to have the right data in your corner.

"If you were a Fortune 500 company, you would clearly hire a team of economists and analysts to track what is going on in email marketing on a day-by-day basis," Thornton continued, adding, "but an email marketer who understands how to leverage AI against sticky problems like open and click-through rates can just take advantage of the fact that AI knows pretty much everything that team would. You just have to know how to access that information."

Whoa.

It's all about *accessing information*.

And who is better at that than email marketers? No one!

Well, no one except email marketers who have teamed up with AI in an effective, productive working relationship. That, my friends, is what we are going to learn to do in this book. Let's keep going!

> *"Wal-Mart harnesses the power of email segmentation to take advantage of a buyer's need that only occurs once a year. This will increase the chance of users clicking through Wal-Mart's website."*
> *Khushbu Raval,* NextTech Today

Chapter 2: The "Grand Entrance" of Artificial Intelligence: A Little History

"Most people have no idea the first artificial intelligence system, called an 'expert system,' came into the market in 1980. It specialized in picking components for custom computer assembly based on a list of customer needs. Honestly, that is all you are asking AI to do today: pick components for your email marketing content based on a list of needs – and AI has more than four decades' experience doing that!" – Charles Ra, email marketer

If we are going to talk about the history of AI, we need to go back much farther than you might think. We are actually going back all the way to the early 1800s, long before artificial intelligence was more than a blip on the most ardent futurist's radar.

Why are we traveling so far back in time?

Because you need to understand why the history of AI matters so much, and there is no better example than a pre-Civil War teenager to demonstrate this. So hang on…

Our story begins:

Sometime not too long after the turn of the 19th century, a teenager named Abraham decided to take his education into his own hands, literally. Even though his family and neighbors called him "unnatural" because of his determination to be well-read and his habit of carrying a book with him everywhere (often reading while walking or in a few snatched moments between heavy farm chores and other manual labor[xi]), this teenager was determined to learn as much as he could about the history of the United States of America and the men (probably not so much the women at that time) who founded it.

Why was this so important?

Because Abraham Lincoln knew at the age of 15 that he needed to understand history in order to be successful in business — he was not yet considering taking a run toward being the nation's 16th president — and that he would not learn it in the little bits he had so far been afforded of formal education.

In fact, by the time Lincoln was 15, he estimated he had spent a total of one year, spread out over the period of time between his 6th birthday and his 15th, in school. Nevertheless, the young man, who would eventually rent a room next door to the Library of Congress and thus continue his literary habit, was a published author, skilled negotiator, and imaginative inventor long before he entertained presidential aspirations.

The key to Lincoln's success as a president and, although fewer people know it, as a businessman, politician, author, inventor, and lawyer, lies in his dedication to reading – but not in the way you might think.

We often hear about Lincoln's voracious reading habit in the context of that reading serving as an independent arbiter of his success; the truth is that the *content* of the books he read was the key. From his youth, when he read George Washington's biography for the first time and developed a lifelong fascination with the Founding Fathers, Lincoln's firm grasp of history and ability to recall it for analysis, guidance, and insight provided him with powerful tools for communication and compelling rhetoric later in his life.

Lincoln's understanding of history – and his dedication to historical study – are what empowered him and set him on the path to truly great achievements.

Your understanding of the history of artificial intelligence will empower you to use it on your path to great achievements.

You have probably heard the phrase, "Those that fail to learn from history are doomed to repeat it." This phrase has been credited to famous philosophers and statesmen for more than a century, and we will do well to apply it to our study of artificial intelligence. By understanding the history of AI, we can better understand how this amazing platform and processor may be employed in successful email marketing.

Read on.

A "Brief" History of Artificial Intelligence

In 1950, a scientist named Alan Turing wrote a paper titled, "Computing Machinery and Intelligence." In that paper, he discussed how to build a machine that could be considered "intelligent" and how to test, measure, and confirm that intelligence. He probably would have like to write such a paper sooner, but prior to 1949, computers could not store commands, making it impossible for the machines to "remember" what they had done and adjust future decisions based on actions and/or results of past actions[xii]. Turing must have already had his topic in mind, however, because it could not have been more than a few minutes after the first computer that *could* store commands went live that he went to work writing his paper.

Five years after its publication, the computer science industry had proof of concept in the works, and just a few years later, the world's first chatbot was "born," a "chatterbot" named ELIZA that eventually ended up loaded onto Tandy laptops where it delivered canned responses designed to make human users feel as if they were talking to someone who understood them. For example, ELIZA might respond to a curse word with the comeback, "We were talking about you, not me." (*She's funny, guys! Amazing!*)

ELIZA was based on the classic human tendency toward narcissism; her responses all were designed to reflect the conversation back to the user. She was a huge success. Many other models followed.

"Chatbots were first developed in the 1960s, and they basically just mimicked the speech patterns and content of whoever was talking to them," explained Todd Geese, digital marketer. "The thing that surprised a lot of scientists at that time was that people loved them. They started telling these 'chatterbots' their deepest secrets! What we learned from the success of that first chatbot, ELIZA, is that we are happiest when talking to ourselves."

Fast forward to today's AI and responsive chatbots, and you can see the potential uses for something that can foster a feeling of confidence and community in every syllable of your email marketing content. The sky is truly the limit; after all, our ChatGPT, for example, is better than ELIZA could have dreamed of being when it comes to storing speech patterns and drawing on them to create compelling conversations or, in your case, correspondence.

"That harmony with the written, electronic word is something AI can help marketers replicate," said Geese. "You can use this over and over and over to get incredible responses and results."

From the point at which it became evident that people would tell a piece of software their deepest secrets, artificial intelligence was the recipient of huge amounts of (sometimes top-secret) funding. That's right: The United States government's Defense Advanced Research Projects Agency (DARPA) got involved and began funding AI research. DARPA was created in 1958 by 34th President Dwight Eisenhower in response to the Soviet Union's successful launch of Sputnik 1, the first artificial Earth satellite, the year prior. Since the agency's inception, DARPA funding has propelled research in weather satellite technology, GPS, drones, personal computers, the internet, and many other technologies. In 2021, *The Economist* dubbed DARPA "the agency that shaped the world," and with good reason[xiii]. Its early investments in AI are having a profound effect on the way this technology works today.

While DARPA certainly spearheaded AI funding, things definitely did not proceed as quickly as the feds might have hoped. Optimistic predictions made as early as 1970 that in "less than a decade" scientists would have developed "a machine with the general intelligence of an average human being" have arguably still not yet been fully achieved. After a period of quiet development in the 1980s and 1990s during which AI experts continued to work in the field but little public attention was directed toward AI experiments or development, AI reached a huge milestone just before the turn of the century. IBM's *Deep Blue*, a chess-playing computer program, defeated the reigning world chess champion and grandmaster, Garry Kasparov.

Kasparov was the youngest world champion in history and considered the greatest chess player of all time when he was defeated by *Deep Blue*. In 1996, he had defeated the computer by switching strategies unpredictably; in 1997 he abandoned this approach and was beaten in less than an hour. Kasparov later said, "I lost my fighting spirit," when describing the match. Many argue he did not lose so much as allow himself to be "psyched out." Some members of the chess community believe he could still have won the game had he not resigned and conceded the game to the computer because although he was not in a good position, when he conceded he was not out of options[xiv].

Kasparov later accused the IBM team of cheating by bringing in another grandmaster to direct *Deep Blue* at a particularly difficult point in the competition. Ultimately, Kasparov could not believe that the machine had won. Interestingly, the IBM team that developed the chess-playing AI program had not expected it to win. Later, another grandmaster summed up Kasparov's response to the loss, saying *Deep Blue's* move was "incredibly refined" and "sent Garry [Kasparov] into a tizzy."[xv] Ultimately, that "tizzy" cost Kasparov his focus, his "fighting spirit," and the game.

The oddly personal response from Kasparov to *Deep Blue* was a harbinger of how we would interact with AI in the future. Most humans are simply unable to view programs and machinery that interact in a way that we view as "human" as anything other than at least partially sentient. This can be good or bad, depending on how the program interacts with the user and vice versa.

For example, in 2015, scientists developed a robotic baby seal named Paro that ultimately was classified as a medical device and used as a therapeutic tool for patients with dementia. The fuzzy white seal was used to help reduce patient stress (and, as a result, reduce the stress on their caregivers), stimulate interaction between the patient and others, improve patient relaxation and motivation, and improve socialization abilities in dementia patients[xvi]. The little robot functioned like a real pet, learning and repeating actions that led to affection from the patient user and seeking interactions like snuggling and repetition of its name.

The "Face" of Today's AI is Constantly Changing

Less than a decade since the development of Paro, a vast array of humanoid robots using AI programming are emerging on the market along with an even greater array of ethical questions about the responsible use of artificial intelligence. For email marketers, however, the concerns highlighted by programs like *West World*, wherein robots are abused and maligned by visitors living out their wildest fantasies until (naturally) the robots "become human" and break out into the real world, are not the point at all. Thankfully.

For us, the point of AI is data. Big Data. And what we (and AI) can do with it.

Today's artificial intelligence programs, tools, and software systems are designed to constantly collect, evaluate, and react to impossibly huge amounts of information about what people are doing, how they are talking about it, and what makes them want to do things again. When that data is combined with an AI program like ChatGPT that is capable of writing in a manner that is (usually) similar and nearly identical to human communication, it opens up huge opportunities for email marketers to supplement and enhance their own email copy and product offerings.

However, you will not be able to outsource your email marketing to AI completely. This is where many email marketers are getting and will continue to get it wrong. Either they avoid using AI entirely based on the assumption that the loss of the "human element" in their marketing will be obvious to readers and hurt their business, or they embrace it absolutely, permitting AI programs to write their emails and sending them, unedited and unadjusted, out to their lists without any real consideration for what the program has created.

Naturally, the key to success lies in moderation. Just because you saved time and did not write your own email copy does not mean that copy is automatically valuable. On the other hand, that email copy and the massive amounts of data integrated into its creation *could be valuable* if you were to apply your own skills as an email marketer to the raw materials provided to you by AI. That is what we will discuss in the next chapter.

The key is not to be afraid of AI, but also to view it in a pragmatic, practical light.

Rich Fedrizzi, email marketer, said it best. "Everyone is pulling the fire alarms and warning AI is going to replace email marketing. No. It's just not. But email marketers who are not afraid to use it are going to dominate this space. Not being one of those email marketers is what should make you feel afraid."

"A computer would deserve to be called intelligent if it could deceive a human into believing it was human." – Alan Turing

"The history of AI is just an amazing journey. We've gone from Alan Turing, who would have had to lease a computer for about $200,000 a month, to free access to everyone with an internet connection." – Jim Callahan, digital marketer

Chapter 3: The Intersection of Email Marketing & AI: Supporting the Email Ecosystem

"AI can tell you a lot of things about what other people are doing, but it cannot give you a foolproof strategy for how those things will work in your business. It is a foundational tool, maybe, but it cannot be the entire foundation." – Thomas Bleakney, digital marketer

Now that you have done your reading in the tradition of a certain legendary U.S. president, you can see that from a historical perspective, the trajectory of AI can be divided into two main periods: Before *Deep Blue* and After *Deep Blue*.

Before the chess-playing computer beat Garry Kasparov, a large portion of AI research, technology, and development was largely theoretical.

After the defeat of the grandmaster, the pace of that research accelerated and areas of study and disciplines became more distinct as practical applications emerged. No longer was it the case that robots, early internet algorithms, chatbots, and strategy/reasoning programs were all lumped together under the AI umbrella without much distinction other than that they were all artificial intelligence. Lines began to appear between the different types of AI and who was using them.

In the early 2000s, the internet marketing (not yet email marketing) community dove into this gradually distilling and intoxicating mixture of research, science fiction, and computer science. The first steps were small, and, like today, there were a lot of marketers who were skeptical about using that early-stage AI in their businesses. Also, there were those who did not feel like they needed it (they were usually the ones who were great copywriters or at least believed they were), and there were those who dove right and started figuring this strange new world out.

The important thing to remember when you are thinking about AI and email marketing, however, is that you cannot replace yourself with artificial intelligence. Even the best AI-powered virtual assistant is not going to replace you. Even if you can use AI to create killer sales copy, that AI copywriter is not going to have the same compelling element as you.

What AI will do for your email marketing business is *power it up* with all of the data and history and response-metrics available in the entire ether of the internet. When you combine that kind of "processing" power with your creative ability, that is where email marketing and AI intersect to create a truly powerful cash-making machine in the form of your turbo-boosted email marketing business.

The 2 Kinds of Copywriters & How to Be the Right One

"There are two different types of copywriters. There are the copywriters who write copy that does not get a response, and there are copywriters who write copy that does get a direct response. Direct

response copywriting is the kind of copywriting you must do if you want to turn your email list into a money-making machine." – Matt Bacak, author of this book, owner of InfoSoft360 & founder of The Profit Coalition

I got started in the business back in 1997 when there were about 10 million people worldwide with "web mail accounts"[xvii] provided primarily by America Online (AOL), Echomail, Hotmail, and Yahoo![xviii]. By comparison, today there an estimated 4.6 billion email users worldwide, and Statista estimates there are 3.13 million emails sent every second[xix].

When I got started, we were not just using email to reach people. We were using direct mail [USPS] with direct response copywriting because there were not that many people online and checking their emails yet. As we started sending out more emails, we were basically sending out long sales letters with links in them that would let people buy.

Honestly, it was my intense study of direct response copywriting that brought me my early success in the email marketing niche; good copy can overcome a lot of other issues with a business in its infancy because once you get your copy right, you can replicate that process over and over and create cash flow relatively simply and quickly. Good copywriting is one of the most important things I ever learned, and it is one of the only things I studied and continue to study today.

Today, much as "internet marketing" has fragmented into dozens of more specialized niches (including email marketing), the term "copywriting" encompasses many more types of writing than it did at the turn of the 21st century. Here is an abbreviated list of formal types of copywriting according to (you guessed it) Google's AI-powered web summary, one of the latest AI functions (at time of publication) to publicly debut online:

- Search engine optimization
- Website copywriting
- Direct response copywriting

- Email copywriting
- Brand copywriting
- Ad copywriting
- Technical copywriting
- B2B copywriting
- Creative copywriting
- User experience copywriting
- Social media copywriting
- Content marketing
- Homepage copywriting
- Brochure copywriting
- Marketing copywriting
- Sales copywriting
- Blog post copywriting
- Advertising copywriting
- Billboard copywriting
- Case study copywriting
- Email newsletter copywriting
- Infographic copywriting
- Podcast copywriting
- Video copywriting

You may feel that some of these categories are a little redundant, and you would be correct. We have left the list as provided by Google's AI-powered search to show you that the power of AI can be used in extremely useful ways (each of these categories linked to websites associated with each copywriting niche), but it also does not filter out everything or make everything it produces easy to read and navigate. That remains to you, the human, to handle. And that's a good thing!

All of these categories fall under the broad umbrella of "copywriting" because they are all, in some form or fashion, seeking to elicit a specific response from the reader. Perhaps the most obvious example would be "billboard copywriting," which is officially defined as "the process of using a large-scale digital or print ad to market a company, brand, product, service, or campaign"[xx]. When you see a billboard on the side of the road, that billboard has been designed to elicit a specific response from you. The response may be brand recognition or something that requires more action, such as a sale. To get that response, someone had to do come copywriting…billboard copywriting, of course.

On the other hand, it might be a little harder to figure out blog post copywriting. Many bloggers will insist they are *not* copywriters. They will get offended, insisting they are "not one of those people who just want to *sell* stuff!" Baloney. If they really mean that, then they probably are not getting a lot of practical use out of their blog. Realistically, a blog exists to educate, but the blogger is educating in order to elicit a response from the reader. That response may be a purchase or an action (for example, a blog about adoptable dogs likely seeks primarily to get those dogs adopted rather than reader purchases), but there is a response the blogger is seeking. That means their blogging content is copywriting content because it is designed to *persuade* the reader to respond in a specific way.

Bringing AI Into the Equation

A copywriter who is just *moderately effective* at direct response copywriting in their industry and in any of these niches is well equipped to become extremely successful, and a copywriter who is *highly effective* in direct response copywriting essentially has it "made" in the email marketing industry because, at the end of the day, most links in most emails are designed and included to ultimately persuade you to do something that results in a sale or other form of revenue generation for the person who sent the email. Direct response copywriting is just the art of first, getting a recipient to open the email and, second, getting the reader of the email to click the link with the decision to follow the requested plan of action (buy, subscribe, watch a video, etc.) already in mind.

So, how does artificial intelligence fit into all of this? Well, one of the best ways to take your copywriting from "adequate" to "highly effective" is to use words and language patterns that your readers find both appealing and persuasive. That can be difficult. You have probably written things before (or contracted out to have them written) and said to yourself, "That's no good. I would never click that." However, truly great email marketers know that it is not about whether *you* would click a link or not; the true test is whether *your reader* will click a link or not. AI can help you write copy that resonates with your readers because AI has more information about what is actually going on in your readers' heads. Remember how people started telling ELIZA all their deepest secrets? Well, this is even better than that because with the information AI platforms have today, people are not even consciously thinking about telling their secrets, they are just "talking" to their good friend, the search engine, and they are using the speech patterns, sentence structures, and vocabularies with which they are most comfortable. Access to that information is powerful.

"Here's the thing: Today there are some 4 billion people who are daily email users, and even if you are only emailing a tiny fraction of that population, you are unlikely to establish true commonality with the majority of your life [all on your own]," said Chris Cordwell, digital marketer. He continued, "The only way you can achieve that kind of rapport is by working in data from a 'hive mind' that is bigger than your own."

Of course, the "hive mind" of AI is not always a pretty place, and we will talk about how to deal with the darker and potentially dangerous elements of AI-powered email marketing in a later chapter. However, suffice it to say, this is one point where you will remain closely involved in the creative process.

Andrew D Cowan, RN, put it this way, "Realistically, AI is getting better and better at mirroring the worst traits humanity possesses. That does not make for a good long-term email marketing business model If you leave your AI copywriter unsupervised."

Maybe not, but with supervision, your AI copywriter can do a great job of taking a decent piece of copywriting and turning it into a powerfully persuasive landing page, subject line, or email.

A Brief Game Plan for Incorporating AI into Your Email Marketing

Email marketing was a conceptually simple discipline in its early days. One simply collected email addresses ("subscribers") and sent email correspondence to those subscribers as needed in the course of business. You could sell products or services to your subscribers or sell advertisers' products or services to your subscribers and generally create a great deal of revenue relatively easily.

The novelty of email as a marketing channel was, by itself, sufficient to generate impressive ROI for email marketers in the early days. Even poorly written emails led to profit. But as the novelty wore off, email marketers found it increasingly necessary to do more than simply "send emails" to their subscribers. Instead, marketers had to write truly *persuasive* copy for their emails.

However, the need for persuasive copy was not (and is not) limited to the text within the email. Email marketers soon discovered that there is an entire ecosystem that must be well-written and well-conceived to generate the best ROI, including issues like:

- Subject Lines,
- "From" Name,
- Landing Page, and of course
- Email Body Copy

Each of these components of email marketing are largely exercises in generating well-written *text*, and this is where AI truly excels. In the next chapter, we will dive into the nuts and bolts of how to use AI and put this game plan into action.

"AI is effective, economical, and easy to use. Why wouldn't you use it to improve your email marketing business?" – Dennis N Durst, digital marketer

Chapter 4: The Nuts & Bolts of Using AI *or* Garbage in, Garbage Out, Pt. 1

"The rule is 'garbage in, garbage out' when it comes to working with AI like ChatGPT. That means if you give AI unclear or wrong information, the answers you get back will also be unclear and wrong. It is just like a recipe: add bad ingredients and you will not get the dish you like." – Matt Bacak

"It's true for our bodies, our minds, and our emails: If you put garbage into the system, you will get garbage out. So put the finest quality ingredients into the mixer when you are composing an email with the help of artificial intelligence." – Michelle Coughlin, digital marketer

At the end of the previous chapter, we provided you with a short, simple game plan for how to think about the incorporation of artificial intelligence into your email marketing. Over the next two chapters, we will break down the two distinct elements of AI-powered copywriting:

1. **Getting the AI results you want from your artificial intelligence program or platform, and**

2. **Using those results to write outstanding email copy whether you are thinking of the subject line, the "from" name, the landing page, or the email body copy.**

This chapter will focus primarily on getting AI results from your artificial intelligence program. Getting those results can be difficult at first because your instructions have to be good in really specific ways in order to get a good output from the program or platform. When you are working with AI, those instructions are called a *prompt*, and they are the key to harnessing the power of AI for your email marketing correspondence.

"The art of getting someone who opened your email to click something inside it is rapidly becoming a lost one, which is a shame since this is not really art, it's science," observed Chad Schulte, digital marketer. This is just as true for the art of getting good content production using AI; the process is actually a science, and it can be refined and perfected to produce reliably positive, quality results, but only if you treat artificial intelligence as precisely what it is: a machine function based on hard science that can help you generate persuasive and compelling *emotions* in your readers.

Let's talk about how that happens. It all starts with your *prompt*.

The Truth About Prompts & Talking to Artificial Intelligence

When used in the context of AI like ChatGPT, a "prompt" is a set of words designed to provide the AI model with enough information to produce the "output" (in your case, the copywriting content) that is needed[xxi]. Without a prompt, artificial intelligence does not know what you want to know or what you need it to create – much like any other writer!

Some of the earliest popular examples of how to use AI platforms to generate content were short stories. Users would ask AI models to write stories in various settings or to retell classic tales like "Little Red Riding Hood" using different writing styles. Like any other writing prompt, the prompts used for these stories looked like something you might have seen in a high school English class:

- "Write a short story about an elderly couple trapped in an enchanted garden in the Everglades"

- "Compose an essay describing what stacked rocks are in parks and why they are bad for the environment"[xxii]

As AI learned from interacting with users inputting prompts like these and the users learned from the results of their prompts, people began making more detailed requests:

- "Design a lesson plan that helps students practice multiplication tables in a fun and engaging way"

- "Write a script for an educational video that explores the solar system and its role in the Milky Way"[xxiii]

The prompt continued to evolve along with the content generated until we could ask for graphic design and, finally, marketing copy, and get results that at least met the description, even if they still needed some work:

- "Compose an abstract painting inspired by rush hour in New York City"

- "Write persuasive copy for a rain jacket highlighting its waterproof features, which compels readers to buy"[xxiv]

Because AI is designed to learn from both initial interactions and subsequent refinements of those interactions, such as when a user inputs a more descriptive prompt or adds certain elements to an existing prompt to get a more specific result, every time you or anyone else using AI inputs any prompt, the entire system learns and adjusts based on that prompt. Over time, AI can identify consumer preferences, trends, and emerging keywords (and provide that information when asked) with increasing accuracy and efficacy. It's just how machine learning works!

Natural Language & AI "Conversation"

When you are "talking" to AI by inputting a prompt, it is important to speak to it as if it were a person. Do not phrase your prompt as if you were pretending to be an old-school "Danger, Will Robinson!" robot. Instead, type words that you would naturally speak.

For example, type:

"Provide a list of keywords targeting parents of young campers who need fun camping equipment for their children aged 5-10 including tents, flashlights, and sleeping bags."

When this prompt is provided, the results are:

- Kids camping gear
- Children's camping equipment
- Camping gear for young campers
- Fun tents for kids
- Flashlights for children
- Sleeping bags for kids
- Camping gear for 5-10-year-olds
- Outdoor gear for young adventurers
- Youth camping essentials
- Child-friendly camping gear
- Tents for little campers
- Kid-sized sleeping bags
- Camping equipment for young explorers
- Fun and safe camping gear for kids
- Outdoor gear for junior campers
- Camping gear designed for children
- Adventure gear for young outdoor enthusiasts
- Camping gear suitable for 5-10-year-olds
- Lightweight tents for kids
- Camping gear to ignite your child's imagination

On the other hand, addressing the program like a robot using this prompt, "keywords young children fun camping" with no descriptive information or instructions about the target audience results in this:

- Child-friendly camping
- Family camping adventures
- Camping with young kids
- Fun outdoor experiences for children
- Kids' camping activities
- Camping games for young children
- Easy camping trips with kids
- Campfire stories for children
- Nature exploration for toddlers
- Safe camping for young families
- Outdoor adventures for preschoolers
- Camping crafts for kids
- Kid-friendly campgrounds
- Camping tips for families with young children
- Nature-based learning for toddlers
- Camping activities for little ones
- Family bonding through camping

- Outdoor adventures for young explorers
- Camping snacks for kids
- Making memories in the great outdoors

At first glance, you might wonder what is wrong with the second list. Well, for starters, many of these keywords have nothing to do with what you are promoting, camping equipment for young children including flashlights, tents, and sleeping bags! Both times, you got a list of 20 keywords, but only using the first prompt did you get a list of 20 mostly *relevant* keywords. Speaking to AI naturally not only helps the program perform better; it also makes it more likely that you will include all the details the model needs in order to perform. Both you and AI will perform better when you keep the conversation "natural."

Keeping the "Conversation" Going with Artificial Intelligence

Here are a few things you may begin to notice as you start experimenting with AI-powered email marketing:

- **Over the course of a session, your results may begin to deteriorate even if your prompts get better**

- **Sometimes, the program will seem to slow down dramatically, as if something is wrong with your operating system**

- **"Messed up" prompts may start coming back to haunt you, especially if you repetitively ask for similar things without improving your prompt**

These are pretty typical problems for AI users, and they mainly have to do with the model getting kind of overwhelmed. Imagine if someone asked you the same thing over and over. It would probably strain your brain over time, right? In fact, that is actually a real technique that police sometimes use when questioning suspects because when we have to repeat an answer over and over, our brain begins to have trouble remembering what we said before. If we are not telling the truth, a lie may become evident with repeated questioning.

Although the AI program is not actually feeling stressed out, it may literally be experiencing stress on the system because of repeated prompts or from leaping from one topic to another. If this happens, the easiest thing to do is just close the window and start a new chat. This is also a good idea if you entered a particularly ineffective prompt and had to start over. Sometimes, you may see traces of that prompt in later responses because the model is still influenced by that prompt. It is completely reasonable and does not hurt your results to just close the window and begin again.

Think of the prompt-creation process as similar to baking a particularly delicious cake or pie. Imagine that you start out with all your ingredients on the counter and you are mixing them into a big bowl. First, you put in the sugar, butter, and eggs. Then, you mix it all together. But wait! You accidentally mixed in 3 cups of salt instead of 3 cups of sugar! The cake is ruined! After all, you cannot unmix the ingredients you already put into the bowl. But wait. Now, imagine you decide that you do not want to waste those ingredients, so you will just go ahead and add everything else in the recipe and put in the amount of sugar you would normally have measured for salt. Then, you bake the cake or pie. It probably smells great. It probably looks great. But when you bite into your first piece, well, it is not going to *be* great because you made that pie with <u>3 cups of salt</u> and about a teaspoon of sugar. Gross. There is no saving that pie. You should have thrown it out and started over.

The same thing is true when you are working with AI. If you put garbage (like 3 cups of salt) in, you will get garbage (a really salty pie) out. There is no way around it. Every time you use 3 cups of salt you will get the world's most appalling pie. End of story. So, if you find that you have really bombed with a prompt, throw it out. You are not invested in that prompt. You need to let it go! That way you will end up with compelling, persuasive, powerful AI-powered email marketing copy rather than a disgusting, bitter mess that no one can swallow.

A Powerful Strategy for Affiliate Marketers

Now, here is a really powerful, secret strategy especially for the affiliate marketers reading right now…

Use the "swipe copy" as your prompt.

Let me explain. When an affiliate marketer finds a product to promote to their email list, that product usually will come with some sales copy designed to help the marketer get the campaign running. You would expect that sales copy to be good because the owner of the product is providing it and they want to make sales, but the reality is that usually this stuff is really, really bad. However, these marketers still provide it because they know that if they do not, a lot of people will decide it will be too hard to sell that product if they have to write their own emails. And the marketers are right about this. But the copy still often stinks.

Here's an idea: Paste that sales copy right into your AI model and let AI rewrite it for you.

Here's what could happen:

Original Copy:

"If you have been wanting to make more money for your retirement but do not know how to make that happen, maybe you should buy a vacation home from us and rent it out to make more money!"

Prompt:

```
"please rewrite this sales
copy for a target audience of
25-55 year old professional
adults who have enough money
to buy a vacation home:

If you have been wanting to
make more money for your
retirement but do not know
how to make that happen,
maybe you should buy a
vacation home from us and
rent it out to make more
money!"
```

Result:

> ```
> "Looking to diversify your
> retirement portfolio? Invest
> in a vacation home with us
> and unlock new streams of
> income. With our properties,
> you can maximize your returns
> by renting them out. Let us
> help you secure your
> financial future while
> enjoying the perks of
> vacation home ownership."
> ```

Now, this new copy is not perfect, and we will talk about how you can make it even more powerful in the next chapter. However, you are now starting from a much, much better place with your sales copy materials and, as the best email marketers know, sometimes getting that little "boost" to get started is all you need.

If you have ever needed a little "push" to get out of the nest and start flying, then AI can give you the boost you need to take your email marketing to the next level. Once you bring your own skills into the equation with that copy, your next campaign could be unstoppable!

> **N.B.** This strategy works with anything that you would like to refine or adjust to suit a different purpose. For example, if you see a really good piece of copy designed to sell gold hoop earrings and you would like to adjust it to sell discounted luxury watches instead, you might input the piece of copy along with instructions to adjust for a target audience hoping to buy luxury discount watches. *However,* remember that just about all writing other than pieces that have entered the public domain is protected as intellectual property. You cannot just use AI's rewrite without checking the results and making sure that you are truly dealing with a new piece of content! We will go into more detail on this topic in Chapter 7: Legal Issues.

Your Quick Path to Artificial Intelligence Marketing (Case Study)

With technology that exists and is freely available right now, an email marketer could very easily visit OpenAI.com, apply for a free ChatGPT account, and begin receiving help from some of the most advanced A.I. technology in the world.

For example, I just logged into ChatGPT 3.5 and entered this prompt:

```
Please write 3 email subject
lines that will help me to
sell my company's widget.
```

Instantly, ChatGPT responded like this:

```
1. "Revolutionize Your
   Daily Routine with Our
   Innovative Widget!"

2. "Unlock Efficiency and
   Convenience: Discover
   Our Widget Today!"

3. "Maximize Productivity:
   Elevate Your Workflow
   with Our Widget
   Solution!"
```

I then asked ChatGPT to write a full marketing email for me based on the first subject line it suggested. Here was my instruction:

```
Please write a marketing
email for me. The subject
line should be what you
```

> suggested in your first idea. The email should encourage the reader to click a link to respond.

The response I received was this:

> Subject: Revolutionize Your Daily Routine with Our Innovative Widget!
>
> Dear [Recipient],
>
> Are you tired of juggling multiple tasks throughout your day, wishing for a simpler, more streamlined solution? We understand the challenges you face in managing your time efficiently while striving for productivity and effectiveness. That's why we're thrilled to introduce you to our revolutionary widget - designed to transform the way you work and enhance your daily routine.
>
> Our widget isn't just another tool; it's a game-changer. Whether you're a busy professional, a

student with a hectic schedule, or anyone seeking to optimize their daily workflow, our widget is here to make your life easier. Here's how:

1. **Simplify Your Tasks**: Say goodbye to complexity. Our widget consolidates multiple functions into one intuitive interface, eliminating the need to switch between various tools and applications. With everything you need at your fingertips, you'll breeze through your tasks effortlessly.
2. **Boost Efficiency**: Time is precious, and our widget respects that.

By automating repetitive tasks and streamlining processes, it empowers you to accomplish more in less time. Imagine the satisfaction of ticking off your to-do list faster than ever before.

3. **Enhance Organization:** Stay on top of your commitments with ease. Our widget offers robust organizational features, allowing you to prioritize tasks, set reminders, and track progress seamlessly. No more missed deadlines or forgotten appointments – stay in control

of your schedule effortlessly.
4. **Adaptability and Versatility:** Whether you're managing projects, scheduling appointments, or collaborating with team members, our widget adapts to your needs. Its versatility ensures that it fits seamlessly into your existing workflow, enhancing your productivity without disruption.

But don't just take our word for it. We invite you to experience the difference for yourself. Click the link below to request a demo and see how our widget can revolutionize your daily routine:

[Link to Request Demo]

Still not convinced? Here's what some of our satisfied customers have to say:

- "I never knew managing my tasks could be this effortless. Our widget has become an indispensable part of my daily routine." - Sarah M., Marketing Manager
- "As a busy entrepreneur, time is of the essence. Our widget helps me stay organized and focused, allowing me to accomplish more in my day." - John D., CEO

Join the countless professionals who have already embraced the future

```
of productivity with our
widget. Say goodbye to
overwhelm and hello to
efficiency, one click at a
time.

We look forward to hearing
from you and demonstrating
how our widget can
transform your productivity
journey.

Best regards,

[Your Name]
[Your Position]
[Your Company]

P.S. Don't let another day
go by without experiencing
the power of our widget.
Click the link below to
schedule your demo now:

[Link to Request Demo]
```

Impressive, isn't it? It's particularly notable when you realize that this required only as much time as was required to type in the brief prompts displayed above.

Obviously, you'd never be able to use this text in your own email marketing without some substantial customization. But the framework is there for a reasonably well-written marketing email. However, you must now take on the task of editing and adjusting the AI-sparked copy to create a truly effective piece of copywriting.

"Think about it: Would you send off your kid's college application essays without proofreading them first? No! Every email you send is probably funding that college education, so shouldn't you give those a once-over as well?" – John Milic, digital marketer

Chapter 5: The Nuts & Bolts of Solid Email Practice & Copy *or* Garbage In, Garbage Out, Pt. 2

"There are five universally accepted qualities of good writing: focus, development, unity, coherence, and accuracy. AI does not necessarily deliver those without some coaching." – Daniel G Krueger, digital marketer

Now that you know how to use artificial intelligence to give yourself the best "jumping-off point" for email marketing, it is time to talk about how to refine the content you generate using your skills as a professional email marketer and copywriter.

Now, before we go any farther, there is something we need to get out of the way. There are a lot of people who read that last sentence, the one ending in **"your skills as a professional email marketer and copywriter**," and they just stopped listening and reading entirely. "I'm not a professional writer!" they are saying aloud *right now*. "I'm just not! I could never write a book."

Okay.

Calm down and start listening to me.

Listen carefully.

I need you to absorb this important news flash:

You are a writer.

Yep. You are. You <u>are</u> a writer.

Furthermore, you are already better than most if you are running an email marketing business, and you are about to get even better by reading this chapter and then *practicing* what you have learned. Do not permit yourself to think that you are not a writer. You are. And it has nothing to do with whether or not you have written a *New York Times* bestseller or published something with Random House.

"There are a lot of people who will just tell you, 'I am not a writer. I could never write a book,'" observed Justin M Naylor, digital marketer. He continued, "Let me tell you:

Most successful writers out there have never written a book. That is not the only way to be successful with the written word."

Much of good writing comes from knowledge and implementation of some very basic writing principles. You almost certainly learned about them in elementary, middle, or high school (or all three), and most people absorb these concepts and then move on without thinking about them very much. However, if you want to write effectively, using some very basic concepts like "main idea," "short, simple sentences," and "style" will be vital to your success. In this chapter, we will break these three concepts down, one at a time, and you will see how your email marketing copy shines as a result of these simple changes.

What's the Main Idea?

Tiffany Wong, digital marketer, tells us, "We all learn about the 'main idea' in school, then we completely abandon this concept when we start writing in the real world. Focus is crucial when it comes to really good writing."

Now that I mention it, you probably remember those exercises: You would read a paragraph or a short essay, then you were supposed to identify the "main idea" of the piece of writing.

Here is an example:

> *Dogs make great pets! They come in all shapes and sizes. A dog provides wonderful company. Many dog owners say their dogs bring a lot of laughter into their lives because the dogs are so funny. Dogs also are smart enough to learn not to make a mess indoors, and some breeds are great for security and protection as well.*

What is the main idea?

Dogs make great pets!

It is spelled out right at the start of the paragraph. Now, that paragraph was not written as a direct-response piece; it was simply written to remind you how the concept of the main idea works. In the event that you wanted to write it as a direct response piece promoting puppies for sale, you could start by (you guessed it), using AI to help you begin.

I started by using this prompt:

> "Rewrite the following paragraph about dogs as a persuasive email that sends readers to a landing page where they can put down a deposit on a puppy.
>
> Dogs make great pets! They come in all shapes and sizes. A dog provides wonderful company. Many dog owners say their dogs bring a lot of laughter into their lives because the dogs are so funny. Dogs also are smart enough to learn not to make a mess indoors, and some breeds are great for security and protection as well."

Here is what I got:

> **Subject: Discover Your Perfect Companion Today!**
>
> Dear [Recipient],

Are you ready to invite boundless joy and unwavering companionship into your life? Look no further than our exquisite selection of puppies!

Dogs are more than just pets—they're cherished members of the family. From small and cuddly to big and adventurous, there's a furry friend waiting to steal your heart. Imagine the laughter echoing through your home as your new companion delights you with their playful antics.

But that's not all. Our dogs are intelligent and easily trained, ensuring a harmonious coexistence within your household. Plus, certain breeds offer added security and protection, providing you with peace of mind.

Don't miss out on this opportunity to enrich your life with the love and loyalty of a canine

> companion. Take the first step towards a lifetime of unforgettable memories by visiting our exclusive landing page to secure your deposit today.
>
> Click here [Link to Landing Page] to reserve your spot in line and embark on the journey of a lifetime with your new furry friend!
>
> Warm regards,
>
> [Your Name]
>
> [Your Contact Information]

So, that's not bad, right? Not at all.

But here is the problem with things that are not bad: Lots of things in life are not bad. Brussels sprouts with parmesan, for example, won't kill you, but do you want to eat them every day? It's your job to deliver content that is fantastic, not just adequate. No one thanks you for adequate.

So, now that we have our "not bad" place to start, let's get to work on making it great. And do not get me wrong: There is nothing wrong with using AI to give you a jumping-off point!

"The hardest part of any project is starting it. AI can help you get started," Bernie Meyer, digital marketer, said. Even the most experienced writers struggle with "writer's block" sometimes. However, email marketers cannot afford writer's block because that writing is your bread and butter – literally! Stephen King, the famous and prolific American horror writer, once experienced such severe writer's block that he did not produce anything that made it into a book for nearly four months! (For perspective, Stephen King has an average release rate, meaning he publishes *something*, of one written item every 20 weeks [five months], and he has maintained this since 1974.)[xxv]

King confessed to the *Washington Post* in 2006, "[This was] a four-month period of not writing, drinking beer, and watching soap operas."[xxvi] Let's just consider, for a moment, what spending four months of your life "not writing, drinking beer, and watching soap operas" would do to your email marketing business. Ugh. Nope. Stop now. It does not bear considering. Instead, let's just figure out how to take this "adequate" piece of writing and make it supernova-level powerful instead.

We have established that while not necessarily inspired, this email is a good place to start, and it does convey the "main idea" that a dog would be a wonderful pet, and a dog from your specific canine provider would be the best of these wonderful pets.

However, this is not a particularly compelling piece of copy. For starters, the main idea is relatively close to the main idea of the prompt, but it does not really convey a sense of urgency about putting down the deposit and is not very likely to instill a deep yearning for a puppy in the reader. However, as far as the main idea goes, we are doing pretty well. That means we can move on to the next element: Keeping it simple.

Short & Sweet Will Win the Day

Back in the early 2000s when email marketing was first taking off, people would basically write long-form sales letters like the ones you sometimes receive in the mail and then copy them into an email and send it. There would be links to click (people soon figured out that readers would not necessarily want to read the entire email, so they started putting links throughout these long emails so a potential buyer did not have to search for something to click) and the whole thing would read like direct-response hard-copy mail. For a while, it worked. Until it stopped working.

Over time, as more people got used to email and started sending more emails themselves, they got tired of reading really long-form copy. Now, to be clear, there are still email marketers who use this form and experience a lot of success, but they are the exception, and they tend to be absolutely brilliant copywriters. Today, if you are not a truly inspired and inspiring copywriter who creates consistently compelling copy, you will not succeed consistently using long-form copy. Fortunately, you do not have to!

Today's reader prefers the short-and-sweet style of email. These emails should be straightforward and leave no room for confusion. If you want someone to buy your puppies, then you need to tell them to buy your puppies!

These days, readers actually prefer it when you simply tell them what you want rather than trying to "clickbait" them into visiting your landing page. In fact, HubSpot recently released information indicating that the ideal email length is between 50 and 125 words! Emails that length receive response rates higher than 50 percent. If you can't keep it that short, try for 20 lines or less of text (about 200 words) to get the highest click-through rates[xxvii].

Now, our AI-generated email about puppies is 174 words, so the good news is that you do not need to cut it too much. However, when going for short and sweet, you need to identify unnecessary words and awkward sentence construction. Below, you can see the email again with unnecessary words highlighted and awkward sentences indicated in bold.

Dear [Recipient],

Are you ready to invite boundless joy and **unwavering companionship** into your life? **Look no further than our exquisite selection of puppies**!

Dogs are more than just pets—they're cherished members of the family. From small and cuddly to big and adventurous, there's a furry friend waiting to steal your heart. Imagine the laughter echoing through your home as your new companion delights you with their playful antics.

But that's not all. Our dogs are intelligent and easily trained, ensuring a **harmonious coexistence** within your household. **Plus, certain breeds offer added security and protection, providing you with peace of mind.**

Don't miss out on this opportunity to enrich your life with the love and loyalty of a canine companion. **Take the first step towards a lifetime of unforgettable memories by visiting our exclusive landing page to secure your deposit today.**

Click here [Link to Landing Page] to reserve your spot in line and embark on the journey of a lifetime with your new furry friend!

Warm regards,

[Your Name]

[Your Contact Information]

Now that we have identified some things that need to be shortened, removed, or rewritten, let's evaluate one other element of "short and sweet." Things that are short and sweet need to also be <u>simple</u>. That means a reading level of 6th grade or lower. This is not necessarily because your audience cannot read at a higher level. It is because reading your emails should be *easy*. It should feel *natural*. Any time a reader has to pause to reread a sentence or rework something that they have just read to figure out what you are talking about, their attention is literally up for grabs. If it wanders, you have lost the chance to engage them and potentially generate revenue via engagement or a sale.

The average American reads at a 7th or 8th grade level. This is why we aim for 6th grade. This guarantees your emails will flow smoothly without feeling elementary to the average reader. Think "leveling up" the reading level of your emails won't matter? Well, consider these statistics:

- 99% of people in the United States can read, but roughly one in five struggle with reading to the point they have difficulty finishing tasks that involve reading and analyzing information

- Half of American adults are unable to read books written at an 8th-grade level

- Most Americans spend just 17 minutes a day, on average, reading[xxviii]

You can see that you simply cannot afford to let reading your emails become a chore because it will be all too easy for your audience to simply elect to let reading your correspondence slide into oblivion.

On the other hand, people who do read your emails are proven to be looking for things to like. That is the perfect situation for an email marketer! True Shift Foundation, a digital marketing entity, observed, "According to the ZeroBounce Email Statistics Report for 2024, 88% of people are checking their inbox multiple times a day, and 40% say their main goal in doing so is to find good coupons and identify things they like. AI can help you get identified as something likeable early and often." This is the perfect opportunity for you as long as you keep those emails attractive, easy, and persuasive.

So, let's take another look at that puppy email. You can see we have shortened things up just a little bit (from 174 to 158) and simplified the call-to-action so the reader knows what they are clicking and why they should do it. We also actually made the reading a little easier than it was, dropping the level to between 3rd and 4th grade since, in this case, it did not make the words appear overly simple. We also changed the subject line to something that will incite curiosity in the reader (especially if they like dogs) and brought a little social pressure to bear with the information that 65.1 million Americans prefer dogs over cats[xxix]. By the way, if you are wondering how we found out that statistic, here is the step-by-step process:

1. "I wonder if there is a statistic that would make people feel social pressure to acquire a dog."
2. Search: statistics about how dogs are better than cats
3. Read the first article, which was a *Forbes* article

4. "Yep, 65.1 million other folks could provide a little social pressure!"
5. Use in email

Check out what we've done on the rewrite:

> **Subject: Two-thirds of Americans agree … [Dogs Beat Cats!]**
>
> Dear [Recipient],
>
> It might be hard to believe 2/3 of Americans agree on anything, but…
>
> ***Forbes* reports 65.1 million pet owners agree DOGS are the best pets!**
>
> You know the time has come for you to join them.
>
> Just imagine…You get home from work and your furry friend is thrilled to see you.
>
> As you relax with your spouse, you hear your kids' laughter as they

> create lifelong memories with their best friend. You're truly at peace.
>
> But here's the thing: Time is running out on our adoptions for this year, and we are seeing more demand than ever. You must act now [LINK].
>
> It's time. Meet your furry friend today. Click here [LINK] to reserve the cutest right now.
>
> We can see the smiles from here.
>
> [Your Name]
>
> P.S. We forgot to mention: Training is a piece of cake! Our puppies are proven highly intelligent and easy to train both as a family pet and "after-hours" security.

Now that we have refined our pet email, it is time to bring that special element only a human can bring to an email marketing piece: style.

"You Gotta Have Style"

Diana Vreeland, a famous editor of *Vogue* magazine, said it best: "You gotta have style…. It's a way of life. Without it, you're nobody."

No, we have not gone haute couture on email marketing, but we do really want to drive home the point that your emails (don't worry, not your wardrobe!) "gotta" have style. The important thing is not that they carry a designer bag or wear the latest shoes, however. The important thing is that they have *your* style, because your email list exists because the people on it want to hear from *you*.

When we talk about style in email marketing, we are not talking about the latest and greatest trends. We are talking about a few integral elements of every piece of copywriting, like urgency, scarcity, and curiosity, and also that "special something" that lets your audience know this email came from you. It could be a certain speech pattern, an "inside" joke, or a funny reference. It could just be that you always refer to the people reading your emails by their first names or that you call them by a name that reminds them they are part of an exclusive community (popular options for this include "Geniuses," "Mamas," and "Nerds")[xxx].

In our puppy email above, we created a tagline, "We can see the smiles from here," and also created a sense of urgency/scarcity by letting the reader know there are not many dogs left to adopt. We removed verbiage from the original email that made adopting a family pet feel more like a transaction and less like bringing home another family member because most pet owners (97%) say they consider their pets to be part of their family[xxxi].

Style is hard to describe and seldom formulaic, but it is crucial to creating a rapport with your audience. It is something AI simply cannot replicate, and that makes it one of the most important things you must adjust when you are working from an AI-generated starter email. "AI is only nuanced if the great big ether out there is nuanced. Think about the internet. Is that a truly nuanced world? No," said Matt

"Shappy" Shapiro, digital marketer. You, as the human email marketer, must bring the nuance, the style, to your email marketing pieces.

Philip Booth, digital marketer, explained, "Once a consumer has some loyalty to your brand, more than two-thirds will say they prefer regular, frequent email communication. That is an email marketer's dream." It is also why your style is so very important. The best way to create loyalty – even if you are not yet in a consumer relationship with a potential customer – is to be recognizable. If your emails are generic and hard to recognize, it is difficult to develop loyalty to you. Using just a little style or "flare" helps your audience recognize you (and get excited about opening your emails) every time they see those emails in their inbox.

"Think about what works in the best marketing, and then think about what AI does. They both get views, but only a human has that emotional edge. That can't be learned, and it isn't going to change." – Matt Luckman, email marketer

Chapter 6: Customization vs. Plagiarism

"Every experienced email marketer knows that our particular legal space is something of a minefield if you do not understand the basic principles of intellectual property. That is where AI cannot help you, but you can help your AI." – Matt Bacak

On April 28, 2003, a young man living his dream of being a *New York Times* editor received a phone call that would send his entire life crashing down around him. What was even more shocking, than the phone call, however, was that this precocious young reporter's actions would send one of the longest running "newspapers of record" in America reeling as well. The reporter's name was Jayson Blair, and, by the time the dust settled, he had admitted to multiple instances of plagiarism and even outright fabrication in his reporting for the newspaper. In addition to losing his own job, Blair's actions (and his superiors' failure to detect or report them) ultimately led to the resignation of an executive editor and managing editor at the *Times* as well[xxxii].

So, yes. Plagiarism is a big deal. You might not be a *New York Times* editor (and congratulations on choosing a much more lucrative profession!), but plagiarism still matters and becomes increasingly important when you are dealing with copywriting because effective, compelling sales copy is some of the most valuable writing in the world. Why? Because effective copywriting is literally the stuff that turns words into gold because people read it, click the links, and then make purchasing decisions that positively affect your bottom line.

"It's pretty straightforward to get a pretty solid open rate for emails, but click-through rate is tougher and only becoming more so," observed Jane M. Lengel, digital marketer, when we asked her about the importance of copywriting in today's economy. As of 2022, average email open rates hovered around 21.5%, and skilled copywriters were able to net open rates higher than 30% with relative consistency[xxxiii].

However, that number has been falling since 2013. In 2013, the average open rate was nearly 30%, and skilled copywriters garnered open rates much higher than this. By 2020, the open rate was just over 21.3%, and it has remained in that general vicinity since then[xxxiv].

Click-through rates have foundered much more significantly over the past two decades, which is problematic for email marketers because click-through is a crucial component in successful email marketing. As of 2024, click-through rates, also called CTRs, had fallen to an average across all industries of about 1%, although average open rate was near 40% in some spaces[xxxv]. While this low CTR is not good for any industry, in email marketing it spells disaster.

The key to avoiding this disaster revolves around your ability to craft compelling copy that will inspire your readers to click your links. And if someone thinks you stole *their* compelling copy, they will come after you because that copy is an asset to their business that they cannot afford to lose.

So, how can we get this valuable words-to-gold copy in the first place, and why are we worried about plagiarism if we are writing it ourselves?

Well, you are writing it, but remember you are jump-starting the process and powering up the persuasion by using AI also. Unfortunately, AI just doesn't really understand plagiarism (although it is learning).

You must monitor AI closely because AI is exactly what the name describes: *artificial*. Its information is ultimately scraped from a vast amalgamation of data and material online, and that means you must be very careful to confirm that the email marketing copy you distribute is uniquely your own.

"If someone asked you if you want Dan Kennedy to write your emails, you wouldn't turn that down, right?" asked Rob Wallace, email marketer. He continued, "Of course not! You would have to be crazy to pass that up! And it is also crazy to turn down access to insight from a program that has more information about trends, statistics, online behavior, and just what works than you ever could. The issue, of course, is that you have to make sure your AI isn't just scraping Dan Kennedy off the internet and putting his stuff in your marketing materials."

Because AI cannot identify plagiarism or pinpoint the place in the spectrum of infringement at which a problem officially occurs, you must review your AI-supplemented content carefully. In 2023, Copyleaks determined nearly 60% of all GPT-3.5 outputs contained "some form of plagiarized content"[xxxvi]. They defined plagiarism as:

- **Identical text**: one-for-one copying of someone else's work that is passed off as your own

- **Minor changes**: making only minor alterations to source material (i.e. altering verbs; slow to slowly) and passing off content as your own

- **Paraphrased text**: putting someone else's original idea into your own

> words and failing to credit the
> original source

While Blair's plagiarism cost him his reputation and job but did not land him in jail, plagiarism is considered a felony in some states, *especially if the plagiarism results in the plagiarist earning money using that stolen material.* Federal law states that if a plagiarist copies and earns more than $2,500 from copyrighted material, they could face up to 10 years in jail and as much as $250,000 in fines[xxxvii].

Now, think about how much money you know you can make as an internet marketer. Far, far more than $2,500, I bet!

Clearly, you cannot afford to plagiarize content, <u>even inadvertently</u>.

Furthermore, in the email marketing industry, everyone is watching carefully for plagiarism because they all know exactly what those valuable, persuasive words are worth. You are far more likely to "get caught" in this space than most others, and you are also far more likely to face legal action because if you copied someone's sales materials, that directly impacts their business.

3 Ways to Use AI, Create Custom Content, and Avoid Inadvertent Plagiarism

The hard truth is that AI will sometimes scrape content too closely. Your job is to catch those issues before they become a problem! In most cases, the best thing you can do is work through the steps you would take anyway to refine and improve your AI-generated copy. A lot of times, this will resolve the issue on its own. However, you should still take these 3 additional steps to make sure you are safely using AI for your email marketing business while avoiding inadvertent plagiarism:

Step 1: Use a plagiarism checker (or two).

Plagiarism checkers are online programs that compare a piece of writing to writing available on the internet. There are many free options. Just copy and paste your email or landing page content into the plagiarism checker and let the program do its job. You might want to use two different checkers just to be safe since not every plagiarism checking program checks the same types of things.

What to do if you fail the test: Make a few more changes! Plagiarism checkers highlight the problem areas, so you will know what to adjust. Adjust it. Then, check again.

Step 2: Look for inconsistencies in tone & style.

Before plagiarism-checking programs existed, one of the biggest signs material might have been plagiarized was inconsistency in tone and style of writing. We have already talked about how it is important to make sure your style is reflected in your AI-generated email marketing content. Look for places where the transition is rough or abrupt. These are the most likely places that you might have a plagiarism issue, and by the time you smooth them out, you should have removed plagiarism issues as well.

What to do if you detect rough or awkward shifts in tone or style: Try to smooth the transition area out so that the entire piece of content sounds more like you.

Step 3: Be diligent and do your best.
Plagiarism is a legal issue whether you do it on purpose or not, which is why you must monitor your AI content carefully. Read through your content with an eye toward details and familiarity. As you continue to grow in the email marketing space, more experts and their content and writing style will become familiar to you. If you spot something that "sounds just like Dan Kennedy," it could well be because your AI

scraped it off of Kennedy or someone else who copied him. When you find this type of issue, try to make small but meaningful adjustments (if it sounds like Kennedy, it is probably good, after all!).

What to do if you experience déjà vu:
Adjust and check again. Unlike with academic papers where you have the option of citing your sources, when you are creating marketing copy, you just need to be sure your content is original. Adjust, then recheck to be sure.

It's Okay to Make Your Copy Your Own

When it comes to customizing content from your artificial intelligence "team" of copywriters, it might be starting to feel like you are rewriting rather than customizing. Do not let yourself become overwhelmed; we are just covering all of our bases to make sure that you are protecting yourself and your business to the very best of your ability. Remember, the point of using AI is not to have the computer "write for you" but, rather, to leverage the insights available through AI to create the best email copy possible. A lot of that will have more to do with more subtle elements of your copy, like keywords, topics, or structure, than it will with any one specific phrase.

For example, AI can help you leverage words, phrases, or even email and landing page structures from especially attractive topics, such as real estate, in your own marketing – even if you are not promoting a product in that niche! "Education, government, and real estate are topics consumers report as being the most attractive email topics," explained David "Howie" Howerton, digital marketer. "Nearly one in every five people who opens an email on one of these topics will click the link inside, and AI can help us take the things that make correspondence from those sectors attractive or compelling and translate that to our own marketing."

To see this concept in action, take a look at the following example:

> *Bill sells a product catering to small-business owners who want to get office supplies at a discount. He has a great product, and this is how his landing page describes it:*
>
> **`100 Rolls for $100`**
>
> ```
> Get deals on all the best
> supplies without being a
> big box-store!
> ```
>
> ```
> We get the best discounts
> and deals and update our
> warehouse inventory
> regularly.
> ```
>
> ```
> Join now! (button to click)
> ```

Bill's landing page is kind of hard to understand, although it is good that it is simple and does not have a lot of distractions. Bill's friend, Lisa, mentions to him that she recently got an email about investing in private mortgages, and she "just had to sign up" when she saw the landing page "because it made the whole process sound like you could be a millionaire!" Bill went home, pulled up his AI platform, and created the following prompt:

> I sell a product that gets good discounts for small business owners like the ones that big stores like Walmart get. I want to have a landing page for people to sign up for the service that emphasizes how much money they can save and how it will help their business be successful. I need the following information on the page:
>
> 100 Rolls for $100
>
> Get deals on all the best supplies without being a big box-store!
>
> We get the best discounts and deals and update our warehouse inventory regularly.
>
> Join now! (button to click)
>
> I want it to have the look and feel of a real estate

```
investing course landing
page
```

Notice how Bill just told ChatGPT exactly what he wanted as if he were talking to a friend. The program responded with two results and asked him to indicate which one he preferred in order to help make the model better. They were not formatted in exactly the same way, so Bill got some ideas about how to design his page as well as what to write on it.

Here they are:

Option 1

```
Welcome to our exclusive
small business savings
program! Unlock the power
of big-box discounts
without the overhead.
Here's why you should join:
```

100 Rolls for $100 ```Secure
incredible deals like this
and more. Our program
grants you access to bulk
discounts that rival those
of major retailers like
Walmart, without the need
for large purchase volumes.
```
```

Access to Premium Supplies
Obtain deals on all the best supplies crucial for your business operations. We diligently curate our inventory, ensuring you have access to top-quality products that are essential for your success.

Regularly Updated Inventory
Stay ahead of the curve with our regularly updated warehouse inventory. We continuously source the best deals and discounts, so you can focus on growing your business while saving money effortlessly.

Join Now! Don't miss out on this opportunity to revolutionize your small business savings. Click the button below to join now and start reaping the benefits of our exclusive program.

[Join Now] (button to click)

Invest in your business's success today. Join our program and start saving like never before!

Option 2

Welcome to SmallBizSavings!

Unlock Incredible Discounts for Your Business Success

Are you tired of paying inflated prices for your business supplies? Say goodbye to overpriced essentials and hello to unbeatable deals tailored for small business owners like you. At SmallBizSavings, we believe that every business, regardless of size, deserves access to the same discounts enjoyed by big-box retailers.

What We Offer:

- **100 Rolls for $100**: Yes, you read that right! Imagine

stocking up on essential supplies without breaking the bank. With our exclusive deals, you can secure 100 rolls for just $100, saving you a significant chunk of your business budget.
- **Access to Top-Quality Supplies:** From office essentials to janitorial supplies, we have everything your business needs to thrive. Our carefully curated inventory ensures that you get access to the best products without compromising on quality.
- **Regularly Updated Inventory:** We understand that staying ahead in business requires staying updated. That's why we constantly refresh our inventory to bring you the latest and greatest deals.

> With SmallBizSavings, you'll never miss out on a great opportunity to save.
>
> **Join Now and Start Saving!**
>
> Don't let inflated prices hold your business back. Join SmallBizSavings today and unlock a world of discounts and savings. Click the button below to start your journey towards business success!

Now that you have read Chapters 4 and 5, you will certainly have some ideas about how you could customize these suggested landing pages to make them even more compelling, but you can see what a great start they are for someone like Bill who was not even sure where to begin when it came to fixing his page!

Dior/Flannel Shirt Case Study on Making Copy Your Own

In some cases, you may want to use another piece of copywriting as a model for your AI copywriter. For example, here is the text found in an ad for Dior cologne that is often cited as powerful written sales copy:

> *Dior Homme Eau de Toilette is intriguingly powerful and appealingly fresh. Dior Homme holds the promise of an intensely woody masculinity that envelops and enfolds, and leaves a lasting impression. A man, yes, but a man of many nuances: confident in both his strength and his tenderness. A raw wood, hand-chiseled by Dior.[xxxviii]*

Imagine you want to use the power of artificial intelligence to leverage the great things about that piece of copywriting in order to promote your brand of flannel shirts. You might prompt AI:

```
Please adjust the following
ad copy to promote flannel
shirts instead of Dior
cologne. Emphasize the
shirts make the wearer look
and feel powerful and
create a feeling of intense
masculinity and nuance.

Dior Homme Eau de Toilette
```

> is intriguingly powerful and appealingly fresh. Dior Homme holds the promise of an intensely woody masculinity that envelops and enfolds, and leaves a lasting impression. A man, yes, but a man of many nuances: confident in both his strength and his tenderness. A raw wood, hand-chiseled by Dior.

The response received:

> "Wrap yourself in the commanding presence of our flannel shirts. Crafted for the modern man seeking both strength and subtlety, our flannel shirts exude an aura of intense masculinity and nuanced confidence. Feel the power of every thread as you embody raw sophistication. Elevate your wardrobe with flannel shirts that leave a lasting impression, just like you."

Now, you may or may not love this copy when it is applied to flannel shirts, but the bigger issue is that you could very well have an intellectual property (IP) issue on your hands if you use this copy as it was returned to you by the AI model. If you want to be sure you are dealing with unique copy, you will need to run the end product (you can edit first since this makes it even more your own) through a plagiarism checker before you deploy it to your email list. Bear in mind, the risk of IP infringement becomes much greater when you use material written by someone else operating in the same industry or space as you are.

For example, if you read a really good email from someone else in the affiliate marketing space and put it into AI in order to "make it your own," you must be very, very sure it is sufficiently your own before you use it. To help put into perspective how serious the potential threat of underhanded use of AI really is, we asked Dr. Adrian Low to talk a little bit about the issue. "Most colleges and universities are actually labeling AI-generated academic content automatic plagiarism at this point," Dr. Low said, explaining that the "safety valve" for keeping content unique is making sure you have altered it in ways that make it suit *your audience* and that do not feel generic. It is not enough, for example, to change articles like *a, an,* or *the.* It's the individual element that makes the difference."

Tracy Grote, email marketer, agreed. "Every email marketer using AI must take this seriously," he warned. "Copyright infringement can cost you up to $150,000 every time you commit the crime, and that's before you pay your legal fees and those of the plaintiff. If you run a piece of AI generated content through a plagiarism checker, you can get up to a 97% theft rate, and if you do not know how to address that issue, you're going to be in trouble at some point."

N.B.I. We ran the flannel-shirt copy through the Grammarly plagiarism-checker and it did not throw up any red flags. Our particular points of concern were the "intense masculinity" and "nuanced confidence" descriptions, which seemed a

> little too close, potentially, to the original ad.
>
> If we were going to use this copy, we might adjust these slightly even though the plagiarism-checker did not flag them. For example, AI changed "intensely woody masculinity" to "intense masculinity," which, absent the "nuanced confidence, does not feel like a particularly unique phrase. For that reason, we would probably adjust "nuanced confidence" to something like *subtle*, *peerless,* or *refined.*
>
> N.B.II. If you ever really like the sound of a word but fear using it will create plagiarism issues, use a search engine to pull up synonyms and pick the one that creates a similar feel.

Now, the time has come for us to discuss some very serious topics that come with AI. These are the *legal issues*. Fortunately, a lot of what we will discuss you have already heard a little about when we discussed intellectual property and plagiarism. In

Chapter 8, we will break these topics down in a little more detail.

"Emails from a consumer-acknowledged educational resource are the most likely to get a click-through from a reader, and even then the average is about one in 20. If consumers recognize you as a marketer, fewer than 2% will click your links, so it's definitely better to have an educational relationship with the people receiving your emails." – Dan Ulin, digital marketer

Chapter 7: Legal Issues You May Encounter with AI-Generated Content

"I think we all know making false claims about weight loss or working from home is a recipe for disaster, but what do you do when your product really does something almost unbelievable? You use artificial intelligence to write the best email possible because it is a crime to keep that kind of light hidden under a bushel, but you also make sure you are abiding by absolutely every letter in the law." – Matt Bacak

For all of you who love watching *Star Wars*, you should thank your lucky stars that the galaxy far, far away managed to overcome a nasty intellectual property (IP) suit it actually lost back in 1977. Otherwise, instead of Han, Chewy, Luke, and Leia (and Rey, Kylo Ren, BB-8, and Ahsoka, and so on...) you could have been watching Starbuck, Apollo, Boomer, and, well, you don't recognize any of those names, do you? Well, that is why you want to steer clear of IP infringement: Sometimes, the winners are actually the losers. It's not a risk you should ever take.

Here's what happened (in a nutshell):

During the 1970s, George Lucas was making *Star Wars* for the silver screen and had hired a visual effects (VFX) artist named John Dykstra. This artist was highly recommended because he had done some really great stuff in *2001: A Space Odyssey*. Lucas did not get along with Dykstra, however, and the artist was released from the first *Star Wars* movie after he had worked on a number of now-iconic scenes and had even invented a new camera technique that Lucas did not like but did later cite as evidence that Dykstra had taken IP from his time at *Star Wars* and used it to benefit *Battlestar Galactica*, another science fiction production about outer space adventures, where he landed after losing his job in a galaxy far, far away.

Both sides accused the other of stealing plotlines, including having a heroine "imprisoned by totalitarian forces" and ending the movie with "an attack by the democratic fighter pilots on the totalitarian headquarters." Of course, movie historians like *ScreenRant*'s Mark Donaldson have pointed out for years that these plot points are held in common with "any World War 2 movie involving the American or Royal Air Forces"[xxxix]. Many industry insiders believe the real reason for much of the conflict was that Lucas, who did not care for Dykstra to begin with, was upset that the artist's experience on the *Star Wars* screen influenced his successful work with *Battlestar Galactica* afterward. Either way, the lawsuits dragged on, and *Battlestar Galactica* was ultimately canceled three years before the two sides reached a settlement. As part of that settlement, *Battlestar Galactica* could not return to television for 20 years[xl]. Ultimately, it did gain a cult following but certainly never proved any real competition for the Jedi their friends. In the end, *Star Wars* "won" and *Battlestar Galactica* "lost" at least in part because the latter simply lacked the stamina and popularity to withstand the lawsuits that evolved out of the two productions' similarities.

IP infringements are a big deal, but not just because you can lose a lot of money if you lose a case against you. They are a big deal because they are complicated and expensive to litigate, often drag on, may put your entire operation on hold indefinitely, and frequently the true "winner" is determined more by who is still in business when the lawsuit is finally over.

The best way to handle legal issues like IP associated with AI-powered email marketing content is to do everything you can to avoid them. The first thing you need to do is understand what you are dealing with. Then, you use caution, due diligence, and your own common sense to make sure you are on the right side of the situation every single time so that instead of an IP issue, anyone considering bringing a case against you will, instead, find a non-issue.

The Four Areas of IP Law

When most people think about intellectual property (IP), they tend to think mainly about trademarks and copyrights. However, there are actually four different primary areas of IP Law. They are:

- **Patent Law**
  Patents protect inventions and allow investors to exclude others from "making, using, offering for sale, importing, or selling the invention in the United States."[xli]

- **Copyright Law**
  Copyrights protect original works "fixed in a tangible medium of expression." This means the written word, musical composition, artistic works, and dramatic presentations. This is where you are most likely to encounter any issues with AI-generated copy, and the waters are murky because electronic and digital copyright protections are still a little like the "Wild West" in IP law.

- **Trademark Law**
  Trademarks are words, names, symbols, devices, or a combination of these four elements that make a product (goods or services) stand out. For example, the smell of Play-Doh! is trademarked. The brand

"aspirin" used to be trademarked in the United States, but the trademark was revoked in 1919 when aspirin became available for public sale as a generic. In many countries, "aspirin" is still trademarked.

- **Trade Secrets**
  Trade secrets are any proprietary information used by a business enterprise. They can be things like recipes (for example, how to make Coca-Cola) or business strategies in some cases. Occasionally, you might encounter a trade-secret issue in internet marketing.

False IP Claims

Not many people are aware of this, but the reverse of an actual IP infringement has a name (copyfraud) and can be as damaging as the real thing. IP claims are often weaponized by individuals hoping to control supply, give their own business an advantage, eliminate a competitor, snag a quick cash payout from a defendant who does not want to go to court, or even avoid participating in a glut in the market by temporarily removing their products from retail by making the IP claim. False IP claims are fake claims and are considered to be malicious actions. However, there is a catch-22 with these claims; even if the claims turn out to have been false, they are still evaluated. In the end, if the claim is proved true, the defendant may end up holding the legal bills and dealing with other penalties. If the claim is proved false, the plaintiff may find themselves in this position even if they did not make the claims maliciously[xlii].

False Product Claims

One of the biggest things to watch out for in your AI content is potentially false claims about your product or service. Think back to the email we generated about puppies for sale. In that email, we used AI content indicating the puppies are "proven intelligent and easy to train." What if that were not actually true? Look carefully at the words we used thanks to AI. They're good, persuasive words. Everyone wants a dog that is <u>proven</u> to be easy to train. But how did you prove it?

If you do not actually have hard proof that your dogs are easy to train, you had better adjust that part because this is what the Federal Trade Commission (FTC) calls "unfair or deceptive acts or practices." Essentially, you cannot lie about your product. It is against the law. You also cannot falsely promote your product as something it is not, so if those puppies are not truly <u>proven</u> to be easily trained, you had better rephrase no matter how convincing it sounds![xliii]

The FTC takes its consumer protection role very seriously, and that means if you mislead customers about your product, there are some very heavy fines. You could face civil penalties, be forced to provide restitution to customers, be charged with criminal fraud and both state and federal levels, be compelled to recall your products, and even be banned from your own industry! Take the case the FTC brought against a huge real estate coaching operation in 2022. Once the FTC proved its allegations that the company in question, called Zurixx LLC, was misleading consumers about who would be coaching them and how much money students would be able to make, the judgement included a permanent ban on the defendants from "marketing or selling any real estate or business coaching programs."[xliv]

Imagine what it would cost you if you were permanently banned from promoting or selling your materials? It would be financially devastating! Just do not risk it.

Seek Legal Counsel

As always, when you are dealing with legal issues or seeking advice on legal topics, the best thing you can do is work with your own trusted legal professionals to help keep things moving and also keep you informed of your rights.

"There are two main assumptions behind intellectual property law that AI is on track to disrupt. From feature films and video games...to a book whose author took five years to complete, the presumption has

been that copyright law is necessary to incentivize costly investments. Now, AI has upended that logic.

...

The second assumption, resting on the consumer side of the equation, is no more stable…. In an era of AI-powered recommendation engines, individual choice becomes less and less important." – Thomas Weber, *"Artificial Intelligence & the Law," Stanford Lawyer magazine*[xlv]

Chapter 8: Evaluating & Testing Results

"If you have no idea what happened after you clicked 'send,' then it really does not matter whether you are writing your emails or your hamster is writing them for you." – Matt Bacak

You may find this hard to believe, but less than half (44%) of all businesses use split testing software to determine how their email marketing strategies are working and which versions of their copy are most effective. This is despite the fact that roughly one in every eight split tests drives "significant change" for a campaign[xlvi].

When you begin working with AI email marketing copy, you may be tempted to fall into the 56% of businesses that do not test. After all, we have just spent pages and pages talking about how good this stuff is! However, the key to knowing what AI-powered content, from the prompts to your ultimate deployment of the copy itself, is actually working is to test, test, test.

There are several different types of split testing of which you must be aware. According to a 2017 article by Amy Gallo published in the *Harvard Business Review,* the split testing method is about 100 years old. It evolved from a simple "Does A or B work better when I control for everything else" and, today, runs online with the aid of a variety of support software programs. Users can test the efficacy of different words in their written materials or analyze the appeal of different fonts and color combinations. The possibilities are endless, as are the programs that will enable you to split test and adjust the results of those split tests with varying degrees of automation.

As an email marketer, you should already be split testing. If you are not, however, don't worry! Just start immediately.

You should be testing:

- Your subject lines
- Your email copy
- Your call to action (CTA)
- How layout affects your landing page

- Your landing page
- Your signature
- Your greeting
- What types of media are included in your emails

The list can go on and on. The important thing is for you to treat this entire process methodically.

The thing is that AI can create some really good stuff, but it can also really turn out the junk. Direct response writers simply cannot afford to assume their AI content is great without testing because the odds are pretty good that it isn't. However, when you get a good one, the payoff is huge and you learn a lesson for the future about how your target audience reacts.

Below, you will find a short list of lessons I learned as a result of split testing more than 18,000 elements of email marketing and how to apply those lessons to AI content:

1. **Subject lines should typically be 3-5 words.**
   Traditionally, subject lines have been closer to 20 words,

which means that AI subject lines will also tend to be longer and include a colon or ellipsis. Today, shorter lines work better, so include guidance on length in your prompt.

2. **Emails still need "driving action phrases."**
   This means someone reading the email should be able to figure out what you want them to do relatively quickly by skimming the email. This is best accomplished with clear directions and short paragraphs.

3. **Your email structure should be conversational, so just one sentence per "paragraph."**
   Most people correspond via the written word in paragraphs, but buyers tend to respond better to emails that feel conversational. Give each sentence its own paragraph

> break. It might look awkward, but it will "feel" great to your audience.

The great thing about these rules is that they are extremely easy to split test! In most cases, you will use the split-testing function in your email distribution system to compare two versions. Once you have a clear winner, refine the winner and try again. Keep testing and evaluating until you have the best performer possible. Over time, you will clearly identify what works for your audience and what does not.

Conclusion

Okay, email marketers! The time has come for you to take all of this incredible information and harness the power of artificial intelligence in your email marketing business.

Remember, don't be afraid to try new things. AI is new to everyone, and the rules are not set in stone! You have the power to apply this "juice" to every element of your internet marketing business, and when you do, the sky is the limit!

Matt Bacak

Sources, References & Resources

[i] Statista.com
[ii] Inc.com
[iii] LeMonde.fr
[iv] Statista
[v] Radicati
[vi] BlueCore.com
[vii] BlueCore.com
[viii] DMA.org
[ix] Statista
[x] Coursera
[xi] The Education of Abraham Lincoln
[xii] Sitn.HMS.Harvard.edu
[xiii] The Economist
[xiv] History.com
[xv] ChessBase
[xvi] ParoRobots
[xvii] The Guardian
[xviii] Phrasee.co
[xix] Statista
[xx] Hubspot
[xxi] TechTarget
[xxii] Formidable Forms
[xxiii] Formidable Forms
[xxiv] Formidable Forms
[xxv] Wordsrated
[xxvi] Mental Floss
[xxvii] HubSpot
[xxviii] Cross River Therapy
[xxix] Forbes
[xxx] Starter Story
[xxxi] Forbes

[xxxii] Medium
[xxxiii] Campaign Monitor
[xxxiv] Super Office
[xxxv] Constant Contact
[xxxvi] Copyleaks
[xxxvii] Citadel.edu
[xxxviii] Dior.sa
[xxxix] ScreenRant
[xl] Plagiarism Today
[xli] Suffolk.edu
[xlii] Cassels.com
[xliii] Spodeck Law Group
[xliv] Commerce.Utah.gov
[xlv] Law.Stanford.edu
[xlvi] 99Firms

Printed in Great Britain
by Amazon